KU-021-995

The Wonderful World of

Old Git Wit

With illustrations by
Ian Baker and Roger Roberts

summersdale

THE WONDERFUL WORLD OF OLD GIT WIT

This edition published 2010 for Index Books Ltd

First published as OLD GIT WIT and MORE OLD GIT WIT

This edition copyright © Summersdale Publishers Ltd 2010

Illustrations by Ian Baker and Roger Roberts

All rights reserved.

No part of this book may be reproduced by any means, nor transmitted, nor translated into a machine language, without the written permission of the publishers.

Condition of Sale
This book is sold subject to the condition that it shall not, by way of trade or otherwise, be lent, re-sold, hired out or otherwise circulated in any form of binding or cover other than that in which it is published and without a similar condition including this condition being imposed on the subsequent publisher.

Summersdale Publishers Ltd
46 West Street
Chichester
West Sussex
PO19 1RP
UK

www.summersdale.com

Printed and bound in Great Britain

ISBN: 978-1-84953-121-4

Substantial discounts on bulk quantities of Summersdale books are available to corporations, professional associations and other organisations. For details contact Summersdale Publishers by telephone: +44 (0) 1243 771107, fax: +44 (0) 1243 786300 or email: nicky@summersdale.com.

Contents

Editor's Note

Whether you're desperate to cling onto your youth or keen to join the ranks of the 'older and wiser' generation, getting old is one of life's inevitabilities. As time ticks by we are all forced to accept a waistline expanding more quickly than our granny pants can keep up with, frequent visits to the doctor's surgery and an inexplicable urge to sport a blue rinse. Despite the reading glasses, hearing aids and false teeth of these veterans, their sarcastic comments and witty remarks show that at least their sense of humour has remained firmly in place – even if everything else has taken a somewhat saggy journey southwards. Delight in the glory of the good old days and laugh out loud at bizarre epitaphs and obituaries as age-afflicted academics, comedians and actors share the trials and tribulations of getting old – some more disgracefully than others! Prescribe yourself a hearty dose of lighthearted humour with this selection of quotes, one-liners and witticisms from oldies who really should know better. It's just what the doctor ordered.

ACCEPTING OLD AGE

Old age is not so bad
when you consider the
alternative.

Maurice Chevalier

When it comes to age we're all in the same boat, only some of us have been aboard a little longer.

Leo Probst

What's a man's age? He must hurry more, that's all; Cram in a day what his youth took a year to hold.

Robert Browning

Old age is like a plane flying through a storm. Once you're aboard, there's nothing you can do.

Golda Meir

Middle age ends and senescence begins, The day your descendants outnumber your friends.

Ogden Nash

Eventually you will reach a point when you stop lying about your age and start bragging about it.

Will Rogers

—◆—

At my age I do what Mark Twain did. I get my daily paper, look at the obituaries page and if I'm not there I carry on as usual.

Patrick Moore

—◆—

Getting old is a fascinating thing. The older you get, the older you want to get.

Keith Richards

I guess I don't so much mind being old, as I mind being fat and old.

Peter Gabriel

At middle age the soul should be opening up like a rose, not closing up like a cabbage.

John Andrew Holmes

❦

I always add a year to myself, so I'm prepared for my next birthday. So when I was 39, I was already 40.

Nicolas Cage

❦

Don't let ageing get you down. It's too hard to get back up.

John Wagner

I'm 59 and people call me middle-aged. How many 118-year-old men do you know?

Barry Cryer

—◆—

Sure I'm for helping the elderly. I'm going to be old myself some day.

Lillian Carter

—◆—

God grant me the senility to forget the people I never liked.

Terry Wogan

He said he planned to live for 200 years. I replied, 'Good, I'll be one of your pall-bearers.'

Angelo Fusco

I'd hate to die with a good liver, good kidneys and a good brain. When I die I want everything to be knackered.

Hamish Imlach

When I die I want to be buried in the
'No Smoking' section of
the graveyard.

Spike Milligan

I'm aiming to stop being an adolescent
by the time I'm 50.

Wendy Cage

I want to live to be 80 so I can piss more people off.

Charles Bukowski

—⬥—

I wouldn't like to die on stage. I'd settle for room service and a couple of dissipated women.

Peter O'Toole

—⬥—

When I die I want to be cremated, and ten per cent of my ashes thrown in my agent's face.

W. C. Fields

I should like to die in Manchester.
The transition between Manchester
and death would be almost
unnoticeable.

Lord Roseberry

＊

When I die I want to go like my
grandfather, peacefully in his sleep.
Not screaming, like his passengers.

Anonymous

＊

When I die I want to leave my body to
science fiction.

Steven Wright

What I look forward to
is continued immaturity,
followed by death.

Dave Barry

BENEFITS OF OLD AGE

Old age takes away
what we've inherited
and gives us what we've
earned.

Gerald Brenan

I have enjoyed greatly the second blooming that comes when you finish the life of the emotions and of personal relations; and suddenly find – at the age of 50, say – that a whole new life has opened before you, filled with things you can think about, study, or read about... It is as if a fresh sap of ideas and thoughts was rising in you.

Agatha Christie

We don't grow older, we grow riper.

Pablo Picasso

One good thing about getting older
is that if you're getting married, the
phrase 'till death do us part' doesn't
sound so horrible. It only means about
10 or 15 years and not the eternity
it used to mean.

Joy Behar

The age of a woman doesn't mean a
thing. The best tunes are played on
the oldest fiddles.

Ralph Waldo Emerson

Autumn is really the best of the seasons; and I'm not sure that old age isn't the best part of life.

C. S. Lewis

As you grow old, you lose interest in sex, your friends drift away, and your children often ignore you. There are other advantages, of course, but these are the outstanding ones.

Richard Needham

It is sad to grow old but nice to ripen.

Brigitte Bardot

The more sand has escaped from the hourglass of our life, the clearer we should see through it.

Niccolo Machiavelli

One of the best parts of growing older? You can flirt all you like since you've become harmless.

Liz Smith

Old age, believe me, is a good and pleasant thing. It is true you are gently shouldered off the stage, but then you are given such a comfortable front stall as spectator.

Jane Harrison

The great thing about getting older is that you don't lose all the other ages you've been.

Madeleine L'Engle

You only have to survive in England
and all is forgiven you... if you can eat
a boiled egg at 90 in England they
think you deserve a Nobel Prize.

Alan Bennett

The great comfort of turning 49 is
the realisation that you are now too
old to die young.

Paul Dickson

One of the good things about getting older is you find you're more interesting than most of the people you meet.

Lee Marvin

In old age we are like a batch of letters that someone has sent. We are no longer in the post, we have arrived.

Knut Hamsun

I've got cheekier with age. You can get away with murder when you're 71 years old. People just think I'm a silly old fool.

Bernard Manning

There's one advantage to being 102.
No peer pressure.

Dennis Wolfberg

Eighty's a landmark and people
treat you differently than they do
when you're 79. At 79, if you drop
something it just lies there. At 80,
people pick it up for you.

Helen Van Slyke

The whiter my hair becomes, the more
ready people are to believe
what I say.

Bertrand Russell

BENEFITS OF OLD AGE

Old age at least gives me an excuse
for not being very good at things that
I was not very good at when
I was young.

Thomas Sowell

———

No one expects you to run into a
burning building.

Sonya Plowman on the benefits of being old

———

When people are old enough to know
better, they're old enough to
do worse.

Hesketh Pearson

If you live long enough the venerability factor creeps in. You get accused of things you never did, and praised for virtues you never had.

Laurence J. Peter

Death is one of the few things that can be done just as easily standing up.

Woody Allen

Being 80 makes me feel like an
authority, especially when I say,
'I don't know.'

Peter Ustinov

They told me if I got older I'd get
wiser. In that case I must now
be a genius.

George Burns

Getting old is a bit like being drunk.
Everyone else looks brilliant.

Billy Connolly

The great comfort of turning 40 is
the realisation that you are now too
old to die young.

Paul Dickson

One of the many pleasures of age is
looking back at the people one
didn't marry.

Rodney Dangerfield

BEING A GRANDPARENT

My grandmother's 90.
She's dating. He's
93. They never argue.
They can't hear
each other.

Cathy Ladman

My grandfather reached a hundred
and was then shot by a
jealous husband.

Finlay Currie

———◆———

Granny said she was going to grow
old gracefully, but she left it too late.

Christine Kelly

———◆———

My grandmother is 92 years old and
she hasn't a single grey hair.
She's bald.

Bernard Manning

It's great being a grandmother. You can send the kids home.

Whoopi Goldberg

———•———

When my husband left... he said, 'I don't mind being a grandfather, but I don't want to be married to a grandmother.'

Viveca Lindfors

———•———

Anytime I appear on television my granny turns her hearing aid off.

Julian Clary

41

What's the difference between an Italian grandmother and an elephant? Twenty pounds and a black dress.

Jim Davidson

Grandma would always take the news of a death hard with a gasp of, 'My God, I don't have a thing to wear.'

Erma Bombeck

My grandfather told me too much sex would make me go blind. He had his glasses on at the time.

Bill Hicks

ROMANTIC YEARNINGS

I used to demand good looks. Now all I ask for is a healthy prostate.

Joan Rivers

My husband will never chase another
woman. He's too fine, too decent...
too old.

Gracie Allen

Bill Wyman couldn't be here tonight.
He's at the hospital attending the
birth of his next wife.

Frank Worthington

You can both be in nappies at the
same time.

Sue Kolinsky on the advantage of having
children at 60

An old man marrying a young girl is like buying a book for someone else to read.

Jim Thompson

He gave her a 20-carat diamond and she gave him the mumps.

Stanley Davis on a millionaire and his child bride

I asked the life insurance man what I'd get if my husband died tomorrow, 'About fifteen years,' he told me.

Bette Davis

A man of 90 married a woman of 85. They spent the honeymoon trying to get out of the car.

Hal Roach

—◆—

The widower married his first wife's sister so he wouldn't have to break in a new mother-in-law.

Tony Hancock

—◆—

I must be getting old. I can't take yes for an answer.

Fred Allen

Wives are young men's mistresses, companions for middle age, and old men's nurses.

Francis Bacon

Marriage is a wonderful institution, but who wants to live in an institution?

Groucho Marx

I'm all for May–December romances, but BC and AD?

Michael Harkness on the marriage of Michael Douglas and Catherine Zeta-Jones

My best chat-up line? 'Hi, I'm Hugh Hefner.'

Hugh Hefner at 72

Here's God's cruel joke: by the time a guy figures out how women work, his penis doesn't.

Adam Carolla

Old? He chases his secretary around the desk but can't remember why.

Leopold Fechtner

When you're 60 you get social security, not girls.

Neil Simon

My wife told me I'd drive her to the grave. I had the car out in two minutes.

Tommy Cooper

Yes, I'm dating again but I can't say any more. We don't want to rush into anything.

George Burns at 93

Liz Taylor has been married so many times she has rice marks on her face.

Don Rickles

The old theory was, 'Marry an older man because they're more mature.' The new one is, 'Men don't mature. Marry a younger one.'

Rita Rudner

GROWING OLD GRACEFULLY

When it comes to staying young, a mind-lift beats a face-lift any day.

Marty Bucella

Age should not have its face lifted,
but it should rather teach the world
to admire wrinkles as the etching of
experience and the firm line
of character.

Clarence Day

Don't retouch my wrinkles in the
photograph. I would not want it to be
thought that I had lived for all these
years without having anything to
show for it.

The Queen Mother

The best mirror is an old friend.

George Herbert

I'd like to grow very old as slowly
as possible.

Irene Mayer Selznick

Let us respect grey
hairs, especially
our own.

J. P. Sears

How foolish to think that one can
ever slam the door in the face of age.
Much wiser to be polite and gracious
and ask him to lunch in advance.

Noël Coward

A woman past 40 should make up her
mind to be young, and not her face.

Billie Burke

Time may be a great healer, but it's a
lousy beautician.

Unknown

I don't plan to grow old gracefully; I
plan to have facelifts until my
ears meet.

Rita Rudner

The easiest way to diminish the appearance of wrinkles is to keep your glasses off when you look in the mirror.

Joan Rivers

Beautiful young people are accidents of nature, but beautiful old people are works of art.

Eleanor Roosevelt

The only real way to look younger is not to be born so soon.

Charles M. Schulz

AFFLICTIONS OF AGE

I don't deserve this.
But I have arthritis and
I don't deserve that
either.

Jack Benny on receiving an award towards the end
of his life

I used to play football when I was young but then my eyes went bad – so I became a referee.

Eric Morecambe

I do, and I hope to have it replaced very soon.

Terry Wogan on people saying he didn't know the meaning of 'hip'.

I've got to the stage where I need my false teeth and my hearing aid before I can ask where I've left my glasses.

Stuart Turner

I got used to my arthritis To my dentures I'm resigned I can manage my bifocals But Lord I miss my mind.

Anon

❧

My knees are on their last legs.

Paul McGrath

❧

Consciousness in my case is that annoying time between naps.

Bob Hope

The old have everything going for them. Their hair's going, their legs are going, their eyesight's going...

Denys Humphries

When I get out of bed in the morning,
the only thing that doesn't hurt is
my pyjamas.

Terry Martin

❦

'Do you know who I am?'
'No, but if you go up to the desk, the
matron might be able to help.'

Exchange between Gerald Ford and a patient at an
old folks home where he was making a speech

❦

By the time a man is wise enough to
watch his step, he's too old to
go anywhere.

Earl Wilson

I have a problem about nearing 60. I keep waking up and thinking I'm 31.

Elizabeth Janeway

They say the first thing to go when you're old is your legs or your eyesight... The first thing to go is parallel parking.

Kurt Vonnegut

Old age means bringing a packed lunch when you climb the stairs.

Paddy Murray

The Alzheimer's patient's favourite chat-up line is, 'Do I come here often?'

Terry Wogan

❧

It's not the hearing one misses, but the overhearing.

David Wright

❧

There is absolutely nothing to be said in favour of growing old. There ought to be legislation against it.

Patrick Moore

The older a man gets, the farther he had to walk to school as a boy.

Henry Brightman

❖

The older you get the stronger the wind gets – and it's always in your face.

Jack Nicklaus

❖

I refused to go on that Grumpy Old Men programme because I said, 'If I go on, I will be grumpy about grumpy old men.'

Stephen Fry

Some grow bitter with age; the more
their teeth drop out, the more biting
they get.

George D. Prentice

There's no law that decrees when not
to whinge, but you reach a certain age
– 80 seems about right – when you're
expected to manifest querulousness –
the coffee's too hot, the boiled
egg's too soft...

Clement Freud

My Uncle Sammy was an angry man.
He had printed on his tombstone:
'What are you looking at?'

Margaret Smith

If old people were to mobilise en
masse they would constitute a
formidable fighting force, as anyone
who has ever had the temerity to try to
board a bus ahead of a little old lady
with an umbrella well knows.

Vera Forrester

HEALTH AND EXERCISE

Exercise daily. Eat wisely. Die anyway.

Unknown

At my age getting a second doctor's opinion is kinda like switching slot machines.

Jimmy Carter

To win back my youth... there is nothing I wouldn't do – except take exercise, get up early, or be a useful member of the community.

Oscar Wilde

The denunciation of the young is a necessary part of the hygiene of older people, and greatly assists in the circulation of their blood.

Logan Pearsall Smith

If I'm feeling really wild
I don't floss before
bedtime.

Judith Viorst

People who say you're just as old as you feel are all wrong, fortunately.

Russell Baker

I'd like to learn to ski but I'm 44 and I'm worried about my knees. They creak a lot and I'm afraid they might start an avalanche.

Jonathan Ross

When I was 40, my doctor advised me that a man in his 40s shouldn't play tennis. I heeded his advice carefully and could hardly wait until I reached 50 to start again.

Hugo L. Black

— • —

I am getting to an age when I can only enjoy the last sport left. It is called hunting for your spectacles.

Sir Edward Grey

Old people should not eat
health foods. They need all the
preservatives they can get.

Robert Orben

I've just become a pensioner so I've
started saving up for my own
hospital trolley.

Tom Baker

If, at the age of 30, you are stiff and out of shape, then you are old. If, at 60, you are supple and strong, then you are young.

Joseph Pilates

❧

If you rest, you rust.

Helen Hayes

Middle age is when you are not
inclined to exercise anything
but caution.

Arthur Murray

You can't be as old as I am without
waking up with a surprised look
on your face every morning: 'Holy
Christ, what da ya know – I'm still
around!' It's absolutely amazing that
I survived all the booze and smoking
and the cars and the career.

Paul Newman

I don't want a flu jab. I like getting flu.
It gives me something else to
complain about.

David Letterman

One of the advantages of being 70
is that you need only 4 hours' sleep.
True, you need it 4 times a day,
but still.

Denis Norden

Each year it grows
harder to make ends
meet – the ends I refer
to are hands and feet.

Richard Armour

I keep fit. Every morning, I do a hundred laps of an Olympic-sized swimming pool
– in a small motor launch.

Peter Cook

❧

Now I'm getting older I take health supplements: geranium, dandelion, passionflower, hibiscus. I feel great, and when I pee, I experience the fresh scent of potpourri.

Sheila Wenz

❧

If I'd known I was gonna live this long, I'd have taken better care of myself.

Eubie Blake

Now I'm over 50 my doctor says I should go out and get more fresh air and exercise. I said, 'All right, I'll drive with the car window open.'

Angus Walker

❧

When you get to my age life seems little more than one long march to and from the lavatory.

John Mortimer

❧

As for me, except for an occasional heart attack, I feel as young as I ever did.

Robert Benchley

I'm pushing 60. That's enough
exercise for me.

Mark Twain

I'm 43, and for the first time this year
I have felt older. I'm slowly becoming
more decrepit. I think you just move to
the country and wear an old fleece.

Jennifer Saunders

Do I exercise? Well I once jogged to
the ashtray.

Will Self

My mother is no spring chicken although she has got as many chemicals in her as one.

Dame Edna Everage, alter ego of Australian comedian Barry Humphries

❧

The only exercise I get these days is taking the cufflinks out of one shirt and putting them into another.

Ring Lardner

❧

My best exercise these days is rolling my oxygen tank around like a beach ball when I get out of bed.

Marlon Brando

If you want to know what you'll look like in ten years' time, look in the mirror after you've run a marathon.

Jeff Scaff

The only form of exercise I take
is massage.

Truman Capote

———

I had a muscle that twitched all day
yesterday. It's the most exercise I've
had in years.

Terry Martin

———

My husband hasn't been a well man,
I've had his prostate hanging over my
head for years.

Dame Edna Everage

There is no human activity which some doctor somewhere won't discover leads directly to cardiac arrest.

John Mortimer

You die of a heart attack with the Atkins diet, but so what ? At least you die thin.

Bob Geldof

Too late for fruit, too soon for flowers.

Walter de La Mare after recovering from a life-threatening illness

When I was admitted to the heart unit, somebody sent me a 'Get Well' card that said, 'We didn't know you had one.'

Brian Clough

❦

The best part of a hospital is the exit door.

Tom Brady

❦

My doctor told me I had hypochondria. 'Not that as well!' I said.

Kenny Everett

The doctor told me I was in good shape for a man of 70. It's a pity I'm only 50.

Les Dawson

❦

The doctor told his patient he had Alzheimer's and cancer. The patient replied, 'Oh well, at least I don't have cancer.'

Henny Youngman

❦

I don't want to put my life in the hands of anyone who believes in reincarnation.

Glenn Super on Indian doctors

My doctor told me to watch my drinking, so now I do it in front of the mirror.

Rodney Dangerfield

Doctors are always telling us that drinking shortens your life. Well I've seen more old drunkards than old doctors.

Edward Phillips

A miracle drug is any one that will do what the label says.

Eric Hodgins

I had a cholesterol test. They found bacon.

Bob Zany

❦

'Doctor, my irregular heartbeat is bothering me.'
'Don't worry, we'll soon put a stop to that.'

Fred Metcalf

My doctor said I looked like a million dollars – all green and wrinkled.

Red Skelton

I went to the doctor. 'How do I stand?' I asked him. He said, 'It's a bloody mystery to me.'

Les Dawson

My doctor told me to do something that puts me out of breath, so I've taken up smoking again.

Jo Brand

The ultimate indignity is to be given a bedpan by a stranger who calls you by your first name.

Maggie Kuhn

My doctor gave me three pills. The blue one is for before dinner. The red one is for after dinner, and the yellow one is dinner.

Leopold Fechtner

I'm a bit worried about my last visit to the doctor. He told me not to start reading any serials.

Danny Cummings

CREATIVE MATHEMATICS

I've told so many lies about my age I've made my children illegitimate.

Jessie Kesson

I would say I was 99, dahling.

Zsa Zsa Gabor after being asked what she would do
if she lived to be 100

If you're 39, tell people you're 55 and
they'll think you look brilliant.

Frank Hall

Candidates must be over 35, and
where are you going to find a woman
who'll admit to that?

Bob Hope on why a woman could never be
President of America

Allow me to put the record straight: I am 46, and have been for some years past.

Erica Jong

❦

Thirty-five is a very attractive age for a woman. London society is full of women who have remained 35 for years.

Oscar Wilde

❦

The worst thing anybody ever said to me is that I'm 60. Which I am.

Joan Rivers

She asked me what age she was…
'I'm not sure,' I said eventually, 'but
whatever it is, you don't look it.'

Sid Caesar

———•———

My mother is going to have to stop
lying about her age because pretty
soon I'm going to be older than she is.

Tripp Evans

———•———

The best years of Joan Collins' life
were the ten years between
39 and 40.

Don Rickles

Looking 50 is great, especially if you're 60.

Fran Lebowitz

I just tell people I'm as old as my wife.
Then I lie about her age.

Fred Metcalf

She said she was approaching 40,
and I couldn't help wondering from
what direction.

Bob Hope

The older I get, the older old is.

Tom Baker

Old age is always 15 years older than what I am.

Bernard Baruch

I do wish I could tell you my age but it's impossible. It keeps changing all the time.

Greer Garson

I believe in loyalty; I think when a woman reaches an age she likes she should stick to it.

Eva Gabor

Professionally, I have no age.

Kathleen Turner

———•———

I'm as old as my tongue and a little bit older than my teeth.

Kris Kringle

———•———

I'm 60 years of age. That's 16 Celsius.

George Carlin

I am just turning 40 and taking my time
about it.

Harold Lloyd, US actor and filmmaker at age 77

I was born in 1962. True. And the
room next to me was 1963.

Joan Rivers

I refuse to admit that I am more than
52, even if that makes my children
illegitimate.

Nancy Astor

Age is a number – mine is unlisted.

Unknown

I'm not 40, I'm 18 with 22 years experience.

Unknown

Whenever the talk turns to age, I say I am 49 plus VAT.

Lionel Blair

We're obsessed with age. Numbers are always and pointlessly attached to every name that's published in a newspaper: 'Joe Creamer, 43, and his daughter, Tiffany-Ann, 9, were merrily chasing a bunny, 2, when Tiffany-Ann tripped on the root of a tree, 106.'

Joan Rivers

I still think of myself as I was 25 years ago. Then I look in the mirror and see an old bastard and I realise it's me.

Dave Allen

No woman should ever be quite accurate about her age. It looks so calculating.

Oscar Wilde

I don't know how old I am because the goat ate the Bible that had my birth certificate in it. The goat lived to be 27.

Satchel Paige

CREATIVE MATHEMATICS

She may very well pass for 43 in the dusk with the light behind her!

W. S. Gilbert

❧——◆——☙

First women subtract from their age, then they divide it, and then they extract its square root.

Unknown

❧——◆——☙

I'm 65 and I guess that puts me in with the geriatrics. But if there were 15 months in every year, I'd only be 48. That's the trouble with us. We number everything. Take women, for example. I think they deserve to have more than 12 years between the ages of 28 and 40.

James Thurber

REGRETS, I'VE HAD A FEW

The only thing that bothers me about growing older is that when I see a pretty girl now it arouses my memory instead of my hopes.

Milton Berle

One starts to get young at the age of 60, and then it is too late.

Pablo Picasso

—◆—

I often sit back and think, 'I wish I'd done that'... and find out that I already have.

Richard Harris

—◆—

Oh to be 70 again!

Georges Clemenceau on his 80th birthday after spotting a pretty girl

Any regrets? Yes, I'd like to have tried more positions.

Groucho Marx at 72

Nostalgia ain't what it used to be

Jackie Mason

If I had my life to live over, I'd like to live over a Chinese restaurant.

John Junkin

My only regret in life is that I didn't drink more champagne.

John Maynard Keynes

I have more skeletons
in my closet than the
Smithsonian Institute.

Ben Jones

Early to rise and early to bed makes
a man healthy, wealthy and dead.

James Thurber

Old age is the happiest time in a
man's life. The worst of it is, there's
so little of it.

W. S. Gilbert

I wasted time, and now doth time
waste me.

William Shakespeare, *Richard III*

IMMORTALITY

Millions long for immortality who do not know what to do with themselves on a rainy Sunday afternoon.

Susan Ertz

He had decided to live forever or die
in the attempt.

Joseph Heller

The first step to eternal life is you
have to die.

Chuck Palahniuk

There's nothing wrong with you that
reincarnation won't cure.

Jack E. Leonard

The only thing wrong with immortality
is that it tends to go on forever.

Herb Caen

If you live to be one hundred you've
got it made. Very few people die
past that age.

George Burns

I intend to live forever. So far,
so good.

Stephen Wright

I don't want to achieve immortality through my work, I want to achieve it through not dying.

Woody Allen

MEMORY'S THE FIRST THING TO GO

I remember your name
perfectly. I just can't
think of your face.

Oscar Wilde

Whenever I meet a man whose name I can't remember, I give myself two minutes. If it is a hopeless case, I always say 'And how is the old complaint?'

Charles Dickens

My grandfather found a cure for amnesia, but he could never remember what it was.

Henny Youngman

It's OK to have sex after a heart attack. But don't forget to close the ambulance door.

Phyllis Diller

How comforting it is, once or twice a year, to get together and forget the old times.

James Fenton

———•———

A woman never forgets her age – once she decides what it is.

Stanley Davis

———•———

The older we get, the better we used to be.

John McEnroe

God gave us our memories so that we might have roses in December.

J. M. Barrie

Do you remember the good old days? And the bad old nights?

Bob Monkhouse

I have a memory like an elephant. In fact elephants often consult me.

Nöel Coward

Remembering something
at the first try is now as
good as an orgasm.

Gloria Steinem

By the time you reach 75 years of age you've learnt everything. All you have to do is try and remember it.

George Coote

— • —

As you get older three things happen. The first is your memory goes, and I can't remember the other two...

Norman Wisdom

— • —

I believe the true function of age is memory. I'm recording as fast as I can.

Rita Mae Brown

Once you've accumulated sufficient knowledge to get by, you're too old to remember it.

Unknown

—•—

They will all have heard that story of yours before – but if you tell it well they won't mind hearing it again.

Thora Hird

—•—

After the age of 80, everything reminds you of something else.

Lowell Thomas

Interviewer: Can you remember any
of your past lives?

The Dalai Lama: At my age I have a problem
remembering what happened yesterday.

By the time you're 80 years old
you've learned everything. You only
have to remember it.

George Burns

AGEING ROUND THE MIDDLE

Middle age is when you're willing to give up your seat to a lady on the bus, and can't.

Sammy Kaye

Middle age is the period in life when your idea of getting ahead is staying even.

Herbert Prochnow

One of the hardest decisions in life is when to start middle age.

Clive James

Beware of what you wish for in youth, for in middle age you will surely achieve it.

Johann W. Von Goethe

I wouldn't mind being called middle-aged if I knew a few more 100-year-old people.

Dean Martin

———————

Middle age is when we can do just as much as ever – but would rather not.

Dan Kiely

———————

You know you've reached middle age when the kids will allow you to pick them up from school, but not get out of the car.

Gary Ryan

Youth tends to look ahead. Old age tends to look back. Middle age tends to look worried.

James Simpson

The hands of my biological clock are giving me the fingers.

Wendy Liebman

❧

Middle age is when you look at the rain teeming down and say, 'That'll be good for the garden.'

Grace Marshall

❧

Women stop worrying about becoming pregnant and men start worrying about looking like they are.

Fred Metcalf on middle age

Middle age is the time of life that a
man first notices in his wife.

Richard Armour

—•—

Middle age is the awkward period
when Father Time starts catching up
with Mother Nature.

Harold Coffin

—•—

Middle age is when, whenever you go
on holiday, you pack a sweater.

Denis Norden

It's hard to feel middle-aged, because
how can you tell how long you are
going to live?

Mignon McLaughlin

Middle age is when your broad mind
and narrow waist begin to
change places.

E. Joseph Cossman

Middle age is when you're old enough
to know better but still young enough
to do it.

Ogden Nash

Middle age is the time when a man is always thinking that in a week or two he will feel as good as ever.

Don Marquis

***

Years ago we discovered the exact point, the dead centre of middle age. It occurs when you are too young to take up golf and too old to rush to the net.

Franklin Adams

***

Middle age is when work is a lot less fun, and fun is a lot more work.

Milton Berle

Setting a good example for your children takes all the fun out of middle age.

William Feather

❈

Middle Age: When you begin to exchange your emotions for symptoms.

Georges Clemenceau

❈

Middle age is when your classmates are so grey and wrinkled and bald they don't recognise you.

Bennett Cerf

Middle age is when it takes you all night to do once what once you used to do all night.

Kenny Everett

❦

The enemy of society is middle class and the enemy of life is middle age.

Orson Welles

❦

Middle age is when everything new you feel is likely to be a symptom.

Dr Laurence J. Peter

Middle age is the time in life when, after pulling in your stomach, you look as if you ought to pull in your stomach.

Unknown

Spiritual sloth, or acedia, was known as The Sin of the Middle Ages. It's the sin of my middle age, too.

Mignon McLaughlin

The long, dull, monotonous years of middle-aged prosperity or middle-aged adversity are excellent campaigning weather for the devil.

C. S. Lewis

You know you've reached middle age when your weightlifting consists merely of standing up.

Bob Hope

Mid-life crisis is that moment when you realise your children and your clothes are about the same age.

William D. Tammeus

Middle age is when you're sitting at home on a Saturday night and the telephone rings and you hope it isn't for you.

Ogden Nash

Middle age is when your age starts to show around your middle.

Bob Hope

Middle Age – later than you think and sooner than you expect.

Earl Wilson

The really frightening thing about middle age is the knowledge that you'll grow out of it.

Doris Day

If you want to recapture your youth,
just cut off his allowance.

Al Bernstein

Middle age is when you choose your
cereal for the fibre, not the toy.

Unknown

Middle age is when you're faced with
two temptations and you choose the
one that will get you home by
nine o'clock.

Ronald Reagan

TIME'S WINGED CHARIOT

At my back I often hear
time's winged chariot
changing gear.

Eric Linklater

George Burns is so old, he has an autographed bible.

Sid Caesar

Bob Hope is alive, but only in the sense that he can't be legally buried.

Steven Bauer

There comes a time in every woman's life when the only thing that helps is a glass of champagne.

Bette Davis

Inside every 70 year old is a 35 year old asking, 'What happened?'

Ann Landers

An interviewer once asked me how I felt getting up in the morning at 88. 'Amazed,' I told him.

George Burns

Time is the best teacher. Unfortunately, it kills all its students.

Billy Crystal

Life is a table d'hôte meal, with Time
changing the plates before you've
had enough of anything.

Tom Kettle

❦

I don't know that my behaviour has
improved with age.

Jimmy Connors

❦

The first 40 years of life give us the
text: the next 30 supply
the commentary.

Arthur Schopenhauer

As we grow older, our bodies get
shorter and our anecdotes longer.

Robert Quillen

You know you've grown up when you
become obsessed with
the thermostat.

Jeff Foxworthy

As one grows older, one becomes
wiser and more foolish.

François de La Rochefoucauld

An old man looks permanent, as if he had been born an old man.

H. E. Bates

Old age is when you resent the swimsuit issue of Sports Illustrated because there are fewer articles to read.

George Burns

Time and trouble will tame an advanced young woman, but an advanced old woman is uncontrollable by any earthly force.

Dorothy L. Sayers

Old age means realising you will never own all the dogs you wanted to.

Joe Gores

Forty is the old age of youth; fifty is the youth of old age.

French proverb

Growing old is no more than a bad habit, which a busy person has no time to form.

Andre Maurois

Age seldom arrives smoothly or
quickly. It's more often a succession
of jerks.

Jean Rhys

The essence of age is intellect.
Wherever that appears, we call it old.

Ralph Waldo Emerson

NOT GROWING UP

It takes a long time to grow young.

Pablo Picasso

Life would be infinitely happier if we could only be born at the age of 80 and gradually approach 18.

Mark Twain

—◦—

Age does not diminish the extreme disappointment of having a scoop of ice cream fall from the cone.

Jim Fiebig

—◦—

The surprising thing about young fools is how many survive to become old fools.

Doug Larson

The older you get the more important
it is not to act your age.

Ashleigh Brilliant

Growing old is compulsory, growing
up is optional.

Bob Monkhouse

You're only young once, but you can
be immature forever.

John Greier

The secret of genius is to carry the spirit of the child into old age, which means never losing your enthusiasm.

Aldous Huxley

Almost all my middle-aged and elderly acquaintances, including me, feel about 25, unless we haven't had our coffee, in which case we feel 107.

Martha Beck

The tragedy of old age is not that one is old, but that one is young.

Oscar Wilde

I've got to go and see the old folk.

The Queen Mother at age 97, spotting a group of pensioners at Cheltenham Racecourse

Inside every older person is a younger person wondering what the hell happened.

Cora Harvey Armstrong

I plan on growing old much later in life, or maybe not at all.

Patty Carey

Fifty is the new 34.

Tom Hanks

❦

Few people know how to be old.

Maggie Kuhn

When they tell me I'm
too old to do something,
I attempt it immediately.

Pablo Picasso

BODILY BETRAYAL

My body, on the move,
resembles in sight and
sound nothing so much
as a bin liner full of
yoghurt.

Stephen Fry

When I hit my thirties I found there was less hair on my head and more in my ears.

Robert Wuhl

———•———

I try to wear my scarf so tightly fixed under my chin that it holds in place the loose flesh.

Quentin Crisp

———•———

I've started to use my left breast as a bath plug.

Joan Rivers

They say you're only as old as you feel; in which case I probably died six years ago.

Joe O'Connor

◆

She couldn't wait to be old enough to get a facelift so she could look younger.

Gene Perret

It is obscene to think that some day
one will look like an old map
of France.

Brigitte Bardot

❧

I'm so old that when I get up in the
morning I sound like I'm making
popcorn.

Lawrence Taylor

Jo Brand's facelift didn't work. They
found another one just like
it underneath.

Garry Bushell

Old cooks never die. They just
go to pot.

Nigel Rees

I've spent so much money on plastic surgery it would have been cheaper to change my DNA.

Joan Rivers

The best way to prevent sagging as you grow older is to keep eating till the wrinkles fall out.

John Candy

A lot of girls would have hourglass
figures if time hadn't shifted
the sands.

Stanley Davis

I'm ageing about as well as a beach
party movie.

Harvey Fierstein

Old age puts more wrinkles in our
minds than on our faces.

Michel de Montaigne

I have a body like a rebuilt jeep.

Ernest Hemingway

I'm in pretty good shape for the shape I'm in.

Mickey Rooney at 58

Old age is when things begin to wear out, fall out and spread out.

Beryl Pfizer

I don't want anything else on my body that might fall off.

Gene Perret on refusing to wear a beeper

Drinking removes warts and wrinkles from women I look at.

Jackie Gleason

I'm so wrinkled I can screw my hat on.

Phyllis Diller

Have you not a moist eye, a dry hand, a yellow cheek, a white beard, a decreasing leg, an increasing belly? Is not your voice broken, your wind short, your chin double, your wit single, and every part about you blasted with antiquity?

William Shakespeare

Old accountants never die. They just lose their figures.

Audrey Austin

―•―

An incurable optimist is a bloke who gets married at 88 and buys a house near a school.

Frank Carson

―•―

You don't know real embarrassment until your hip sets off a metal detector.

Ross McGuinness

You know you're getting old when everything hurts. And what doesn't hurt doesn't work.

Hy Gardner

I don't want to end up in an old folk's home wearing incompetence pads. I'm still compost mentis.

Harriet Wynn

Many of us are at the 'metallic' age – gold in our teeth, silver in our hair, and lead in our pants.

Unknown

It's been said that if you're not radical at 20, you have no heart; if you're still radical at 40, you have no brain. Of course, either way, at 60 you usually have no teeth.

Bill Maher

They say that age is all in your mind. The trick is keeping it from creeping down into your body.

Unknown

I don't need you to remind me of my age, I have a bladder to do that for me.

Stephen Fry

Life begins at 40 – but so do fallen arches, rheumatism, faulty eyesight, and the tendency to tell a story to the same person three or four times.

Helen Rowland

Advanced old age is when you sit in a rocking chair and can't get it going.

Eliakim Katz

Everything slows down with age, except the time it takes cake and ice cream to reach your hips.

John Wagner

I knew I was going bald
when it was taking
longer and longer to
wash my face.

Harry Hill

My friend George has false teeth –
with braces on them.

Steven Wright

—◆—

I don't feel 80. In fact I don't feel
anything until noon, then it's time
for my nap.

Bob Hope

—◆—

They talk about the economy this
year. Hey, my hairline is in recession,
my waistline is in inflation. Altogether,
I'm in a depression.

Rick Majerus

BODILY BETRAYAL

It's extraordinary. My mother doesn't need glasses at all and here I am at 52, 56 – well, whatever age I am – and can't see a thing.

Queen Elizabeth II

❧

Wrinkles should merely indicate where smiles have been.

Mark Twain

❧

35 is when you finally get your head together and your body starts falling apart.

Caryn Leschen

My grandma told me, 'The good news is, after menopause the hair on your legs gets really thin and you don't have to shave any more. Which is great because it means you have more time to work on your new moustache.'

Karen Haber

Robert Redford used to be such a handsome man and now look at him: everything has dropped, expanded and turned a funny colour.

George Best

After a certain number of years our faces become our biographies.

Cynthia Ozick

I have the body of an 18 year old. I keep it in the fridge.

Spike Milligan

Thoughtfulness begets wrinkles.

Charles Dickens

I had a job selling hearing aids from door to door. It wasn't easy, because your best prospects never answered.

Bob Monkhouse

Beauty and ugliness disappear
equally under the wrinkles of age; one
is lost in them, the other hidden.

Jonathan Petit Senn

———◆———

Like a lot of fellows around here, I
have a furniture problem. My chest
has fallen into my drawers.

Billy Casper

At 75, I sleep like a log. I never have to get up in the middle of the night to go to the bathroom. I go in the morning. Every morning, like clockwork, at 7 a.m., I pee. Unfortunately, I don't wake up till 8.

Harry Beckworth

Alas, after a certain age every man is responsible for his face.

Albert Camus

I'm at an age where my back goes out
more than I do.

Phyllis Diller

Grey hair is God's graffiti.

Bill Cosby

I used to think I'd like less grey hair.
Now I'd like more of it.

Richie Benaud

———————

I recently had my annual physical
examination, which I get once every
seven years, and when the nurse
weighed me, I was shocked to discover
how much stronger the Earth's
gravitational pull has become
since 1990.

Dave Barry

RETIREMENT

When you're not
interested in trying new
things, that's when you
should start hitting
golf balls.

Clint Eastwood

Americans hardly ever retire from business. They're either carried out feet first or they jump from a window.

A. L. Goodhart

❧

I want to retire at 50. I want to play cricket and geriatric football and sing in the choir.

Neil Kinnock

❧

It's too late for me to retire now.

Michael Caine at 70

I'm retired, but it's an Irish retirement so I have to work to support it.

Dave Allen

———•———

I wasn't very flattered by the boss on my retirement day. He said he wasn't so much losing a worker as gaining a parking space.

Fred Allen

———•———

Lady Bancroft and I have 80,000 golden reasons for retiring, and every one of them is lodged in the bank.

Squire Bancroft

You don't need to retire as an actor. There are lots of parts you can play lying in bed and in wheelchairs.

Judi Dench

An insurance salesman just signed me up for a marvellous retirement policy. If I keep up the payments for ten years, he can retire.

Fred Metcalf

People ought to retire at 40 when they feel over-used and go back to work at 65 when they feel useless.

Sister Carol Anne O'Marie

Retired is being tired twice... first
tired of working, then tired of not.

Richard Armour

— • —

It's very hard to make a home for a
man if he's always in it.

Winifred Kirkland

— • —

I don't want to retire. I'm not that
good at crossword puzzles.

Norman Mailer

When men reach their sixties and retire, they go to pieces. Women go right on cooking.

Gail Sheehy

My parents live in a retirement community, which is basically a minimum-security prison with a golf course.

Joel Warshaw

When a man retires his wife gets twice
the husband but only half the income.

Chi Chi Rodriguez

When a man falls into his anecdotage,
it is a sign for him to retire from
the world.

Benjamin Disraeli

We spend our lives on the run: we get up by the clock, eat and sleep by the clock, get up again, go to work – and then we retire. And what do they give us? A bloody clock.

Dave Allen

The best time to start thinking about your retirement is before the boss does.

Unknown

Don't retire, retread!

Robert Otterbourg

RETIREMENT

The trouble with retirement is that you never get a day off.

Abe Lemons

I'm 42 around the chest, 52 around the waist, 92 around the golf course and a nuisance around the house.

Groucho Marx

Once it was impossible to find any Bond villains older than myself, I retired.

Roger Moore

SECRETS OF LONGEVITY

You can live to be a
hundred if you give up
all the things that make
you want to live to be
a hundred.

Woody Allen

The secret of staying young is to live honestly, eat slowly and lie about your age.

Lucille Ball

I've found a formula for avoiding these exaggerated fears of age; you take care of every day – let the calendar take care of the years.

Ed Wynn

Interviewer: 'You've reached the ripe old age of 121. What do you expect the future will be like?'
'Very short.'

Jeanne Calment

Every one desires to live long, but no one would be old.

Jonathan Swift

—•—

My first advice on how not to grow old would be to choose your ancestors carefully.

Bertrand Russell

—•—

The fountain of youth is a mixture of gin and vermouth.

Cole Porter

Old age is like everything else. To make a success of it, you've got to start young.

Theodore Roosevelt

The trick is growing up without growing old.

Casey Stengel

It's a good idea to obey all the rules when you're young just so you'll have the strength to break them when you're old.

Mark Twain

Ageing seems to be the only available way to live a long life.

Daniel Francois Esprit Auber

———•———

I'll tell ya how to stay young: Hang around with older people.

Bob Hope

———•———

Age is getting to know all the ways the world turns, so that if you cannot turn the world the way you want, you can at least get out of the way so you won't get run over.

Miriam Makeba

The idea is to die young as late
as possible.

Ashley Montagu

———•———

A man 90 years old was asked to
what he attributed his longevity. I
reckon, he said, with a twinkle in his
eye, it's because most nights I went to
bed and slept when I should have sat
up and worried.

Dorothea Kent

———•———

Age is a question of mind over matter.
If you don't mind, it doesn't matter!

Mark Twain

A man's only as old as
the woman he feels.

Groucho Marx

Since people are going to be living longer and getting older, they'll just have to learn how to be babies longer.

Andy Warhol

———•———

The great secret that all old people share is that you really haven't changed in 70 or 80 years. Your body changes, but you don't change at all. And that, of course, causes great confusion.

Doris Lessing

———•———

More people would live to a ripe old age if they weren't too busy providing for it.

Unknown

I can only assume that it is largely due to the accumulation of toasts to my health over the years that I am still enjoying a fairly satisfactory state of health and have reached such an unexpectedly great age.

Prince Philip

Old age is no place for sissies.

Bette Davis

On her 107th birthday she attributed her great age to the fact that she'd never had a boyfriend.

The Star

To stop ageing – keep
on raging.

Michael Forbes

Whenever anyone asks myself and my wife if we have any children I say, 'Yes, one boy aged 44.'

Tony Hancock... at 44

———

Why have I lived so long? Jack Daniels and not taking shit from the press.

Frank Sinatra

———

My parents have been married for 55 years. The secret to their longevity? Outlasting your opponent.

Cathy Ladman

He was either a man of 150 who was
rather young for his years, or a man of
about 110 who had been aged
by trouble.

P.G. Wodehouse

A very old twelve.

Nöel Coward after being asked what age a woman
looked after a facelift.

People say I'm into my second
childhood. The reality is that I never
left my first one.

Spike Milligan

Good cheekbones are
the brassiere of old age.

Barbara de Portago

SENILITY

They tell you that you'll lose your mind when you grow older. What they don't tell you is that you won't miss it very much.

Malcolm Cowley

SENILITY

My experience is that as soon as people are old enough to know better, they don't know anything at all.

Oscar Wilde

How the hell should I know? Most of the people my age are dead. You could look it up.

Casey Stengel

When you become senile, you won't know it.

Bill Cosby

When I was young I was called a rugged individualist. When I was in my fifties I was considered eccentric. Here I am doing and saying the same things I did then and I'm labelled senile.

George Burns

❧

I am in the prime of senility.

Benjamin Franklin

❧

They say that after the age of 20 you lose 50,000 brain cells a day. I don't believe it. I think it's much more.

Ned Sherrin

SENIOR SEX

It's sex, not youth, that's
wasted on the young.

Janet Harris

In my thirties I was doing it. In my forties I was organising it. Now, unfortunately, I can only talk about it.

Former brothel madam Cynthia Payne in 2004

My best contraceptive these days is taking my clothes off in front of my husband.

Phyllis Diller

Everything that goes up must come down. But there comes a time when not everything that's down can come up.

George Burns

When you get older your body changes. Now I groan louder after a meal than I do after an orgasm.

Joel Warshaw

Her husband didn't hold anything against her. He was too old.

Jim Davidson

So Rod Stewart got married again. Where's he going on honeymoon – Viagra Falls?

Gordon McDonald

Why do we talk about dirty old men, but never dirty old women?

Dave Allen

Virility at 21 is considered lechery at 71.

Dr George Giarchi

❦

Are there sexy dead ones?

Sean Connery after being informed he was voted
'The Sexiest Man Alive' in a poll.

❦

Sex in the sixties is great, but improves if you pull over to the side of the road.

Johnny Carson

Old age is an excellent time for outrage. My goal is to say or do at least one outrageous thing every week.

Maggie Kuhn

A medical report states that the human male is physically capable of enjoying sex up to and even beyond the age of 80. Not as a participant, of course...

Denis Norden

Don't worry about temptation as you grow older, it starts avoiding you.

Winston Churchill

I've always thought that the stereotype of the dirty old man is really the creation of a dirty young man who wants the field to himself.

Hugh Downs

I can still enjoy sex at 75. I live at 76, so it's no distance.

Bob Monkhouse

The older one grows, the more one likes indecency.

Virginia Woolf

SENIOR SEX

I'm 78 but I still use a condom when I have sex. I can't take the damp.

Alan Gregory

———•———

I suspect most self-described 18-year-old Scandinavian women named Inga who collect and wear string bikinis are, in reality, more likely to be middle-aged, potbellied guys named Lou who collect and wear string cheese.

Pat Sajak

———•———

After being told his flies were undone: No matter. The dead bird does not fall out of the nest.

Winston Churchill

Sex manual for the more mature – 'How to tell an orgasm from a heart attack!'

Unknown

ARGHH

Middle age is when a guy keeps turning off the lights for economical rather then romantic reasons.

Lillian Carter

What most persons consider as virtue, after the age of 40 is simply a loss of energy.

François Voltaire

There is no pleasure worth forgoing just for an extra three years in the geriatric ward.

John Mortimer

Now that I'm 78, I do Tantric sex because it's very slow. My favourite position is called the plumber. You stay in all day but nobody comes.

John Mortimer

After a man passes 60, his mischief is mainly in his head.

Edgar Watson Howe

Talk about getting old. I was getting
dressed and a peeping tom looked
in the window, took a look and pulled
down the shade.

Joan Rivers

Old age likes indecency. It's a sign
of life.

Mason Cooley

Of all the faculties, the last to leave
us is sexual desire. That means
that long after wearing bifocals and
hearing aids, we'll still be making love.
We just won't know with whom.

Jack Paar

THE GOLDEN AGE OF HOLLYWOOD

In Hollywood sometimes you're dead before you're dead.

Spencer Tracy

Nowadays when a fan runs up to me it's not to get my autograph but to have a better look at my wrinkles.

Liz Taylor

⚬

People say, 'Gosh, doesn't Teri Hatcher look amazing for 42?' Hello – I've got clothes older than that.

Joan Collins

⚬

When Marlene Dietrich complained to her photographer that he wasn't making her look as beautiful as he used to, he told her, 'I'm sorry Marlene, but I'm seven years older now.'

Michael Harkness

An actress once said to Rosalind Russell, 'I dread the thought of 45.' Russell looked at her and said, 'Why – what happened?'

Steven Bauer

—•—

I haven't had a hit film since Joan Collins was a virgin.

Burt Reynolds

—•—

I remember what someone of 60 looked like when I was a kid. They didn't look like me.

Jack Nicholson

The only whistles I get
these days are from the
tea kettle.

Raquel Welch

Why do I never go to the Cannes Film Festival? Because it's full of people I hoped were dead.

Dirk Bogarde

Catherine Zeta-Jones raised a few eyebrows with her flirty behaviour with actor Sean Connery, a man old enough to be her husband.

Martin Clunes

Joan Collins' career is a testament to menopausal chic.

Erica Jong

Old Cary Grant Fine. How You?

Cary Grant replying to a telegram that went, 'How Old Cary Grant?'

Old film directors never die – they just fade to black.

Audrey Austin

I'm never quite sure whether I'm one of the cinema's elder statesmen or just the oldest whore on the beat.

Joseph L. Mankiewicz

YOU KNOW YOU'RE GETTING OLD WHEN...

You know you're getting old when the girl you smile at thinks you're one of her father's friends.

Alan Murray

You know you're getting old when
you get winded playing cards.

George Burns

You know you're getting older when
the policemen start looking younger.

Arnold Bennett

You're getting old when the gleam in
your eyes is from the sun hitting
your bifocals.

Herbert Prochnow

You know you're getting old when you go back to your class reunion and they serve prune punch.

Chi Chi Rodriguez

When he first started going to school, history wasn't even a subject.

Mort Sahl on Bob Hope

You know you're getting old when your 'get up and go' just got up and went.

Brendan Grace

You try and straighten out the
wrinkles in your socks and discover
you're not wearing any.

Leonard Knott

You know you're getting old when
people tell you how well you look.

Alan King

You know you're old if they have discontinued your blood type.

Phyllis Diller

The ageing process has you firmly in its grasp if you never get the urge to throw a snowball.

Doug Larson

It's a sign of age if you feel like the morning after the night before and you haven't been anywhere.

Unknown

Grandmother, as she gets older,
is not fading, but becoming more
concentrated.

Paulette Alden

You're an old-timer if you can
remember when setting the world on
fire was a figure of speech.

Franklin P. Jones

Old age is when the liver spots show
through your gloves.

Phyllis Diller

251

One day you look in the mirror and realise the face you are shaving is your father's.

Robert Harris

One of the signs of old age is that you have to carry your senses around in your handbag – glasses, hearing aids, dentures etc.

Kurt Strauss

You know you are getting old when the candles cost more than the cake.

Bob Hope

A man loses his illusions first, his teeth second, and his follies last.

Helen Rowland

Old age comes on suddenly, and not gradually as is first thought.

Emily Dickinson

I'm getting on. I'm now equipped with a snooze button.

Denis Norden

There is only one cure for grey. It was invented by a Frenchman. It is called the guillotine.

P. G. Wodehouse

You know you're getting old when your idea of a hot, flaming desire is a barbecued steak.

Victoria Fabiano

You know you're getting older when
the first thing you do after you're
done eating is look for a place to
lie down.

Louie Anderson

———◆———

You know you're getting old when
you look at a beautiful 19-year-old girl
and you find yourself thinking, 'Gee, I
wonder what her mother looks like.'

Unknown

Inflation is when you pay fifteen dollars for the ten-dollar haircut you used to get for five dollars when you had hair.

Sam Ewing

The first sign of maturity is the discovery that the volume knob also turns to the left.

Jerry M. Wright

First, you forget names, then you forget faces. Next, you forget to pull your zipper up and finally you forget to pull it down.

Leo Rosenberg

You know you're getting old when all the names in your black book have M.D. after them.

Arnold Palmer

———•———

You're not old until it takes you longer to rest up than it does to get tired.

Phog Allen

———•———

You know you're getting older if you have more fingers than real teeth.

Rodney Dangerfield

STYLE

Age becomes reality when you hear someone refer to 'that attractive young woman standing next to the woman in the green dress,' and you find that you're the one in the green dress.

Lois Wyse

My dad's pants kept creeping up on him. By 65 he was just a pair of pants and a head.

Jeff Altman

———•———

If you really want to annoy your glamorous, well-preserved 42- year-old auntie, say, 'I bet you were really pretty when you were young.'

Lily Savage, alter ego of British comedian and television presenter Paul O'Grady

———•———

You know you're getting old when you're dashing through Marks and Spencer's, spot a pair of Dr Scholl's sandals, stop, and think, hmm, they look comfy.

Victoria Wood

TALKING 'BOUT THE GENERATIONS

At the age of 20, we don't care what the world thinks of us; at 30 we worry about what it is thinking of us; at 40, we discover that it wasn't thinking of us at all.

Unknown

TALKING 'BOUT THE GENERATIONS

My generation thought 'fast food' was something you ate during Lent, a 'Big Mac' was an oversized raincoat and 'crumpet' was something you had for tea. 'Sheltered accommodation' was a place where you waited for a bus, 'timesharing' meant togetherness and you kept 'coke' in the coal house.

Joan Collins

❖

It's hard for me to get used to these changing times. I can remember when the air was clean and sex was dirty.

George Burns

❖

There are three periods in life: youth, middle age and 'how well you look'.

Nelson Rockefeller

Girls used to come up to me and say, 'My sister loves you.' Now girls come up to me and say, 'My mother loves you.'

Lee Mazzilli

❧ ⋅ ❧

Youth is the time of getting, middle age of improving, and old age of spending.

Anne Bradstreet

❧ ⋅ ❧

Parents often talk about the younger generation as if they didn't have anything to do with it.

Dr Haim Ginott

Wrinkles are hereditary. Parents get them from their children.

Doris Day

At 16 I was stupid, confused and indecisive. At 25 I was wise, self-confident, prepossessing and assertive. At 45 I am stupid, confused, insecure and indecisive. Who would have supposed that maturity is only a short break in adolescence?

Jules Feiffer

Young people tell what they are doing, old people what they have done and fools what they wish to do.

French proverb

Why do grandparents and grandchildren get along so well? They have the same enemy – the mother.

Claudette Colbert

— • —

When you are about 35 years old, something terrible always happens to music.

Steve Race

— • —

There are three stages in an actor's career: Who is John Amos? Get me John Amos. Get me a young John Amos.

John Amos

There are only three ages for women in Hollywood – Babe, District Attorney, and Driving Miss Daisy.

Goldie Hawn

My nan said, 'What do you mean when you say the computer went down on you?'

Joseph Longthorne

There are three stages of man: he believes in Santa Claus; he does not believe in Santa Claus; he is Santa Claus.

Bob Phillips

At 20 years of age the will reigns; at 30 the wit; at 40 the judgement.

Benjamin Franklin

❦

In case you're worried about what's going to become of the younger generation, it's going to grow up and start worrying about the younger generation.

Roger Allen

❦

No matter how old a mother is she watches her middle-aged children for signs of improvement.

Florida Scott Maxwell

The children despise their parents until the age of 40, when they suddenly become just like them – thus preserving the system.

Quentin Crewe, British writer on British upper class

Be kind to your kids, they'll be choosing your nursing home.

Unknown

The first half of our life is ruined by our parents – and the second half by our children.

Clarence Darrow

FROM HERE TO ETERNITY

Them that does all the talk about how nice it is in the next world, I don't see them in any great hurry to get there.

Brendan Behan

Death is all in the mind, really. Once you're dead you forget all about it.

Jack Trevor-Storey

It's a funny old world. A man is lucky to get out of it alive.

W. C. Fields

I believe in life after death, which is strange, because at one time I didn't believe in life after birth.

Ozzy Osbourne

If people really believe that death leads to eternal bliss, why do they wear seatbelts?

Doug Stanhope

When men grow virtuous in their old age, they only make a sacrifice to God of the devil's leavings.

Alexander Pope

I think the resurrection of the body, unless much improved in construction, is a mistake.

Evelyn Underhill

The prospect of everlasting life is vaguely disconcerting, and you could end up sharing a cloud with your bank manager.

Joe O'Connor

All men are cremated equal.

Ben Elton

I've had so many things done to my body, when I die God won't even recognise me.

Phyllis Diller

271

For Catholics, death is
a promotion.

Bob Fosse

Death can be as simple as falling off a log. Which is why you should steer clear of logs.

Guy Browning

My interest in the next life is purely academic.

Brendan Behan

If they don't have chocolate in heaven I'm not going.

Roseanne Barr

Any man who has $10,000 left when he dies is a failure.

Errol Flynn

I don't want to go to heaven if you have to stand all the time.

Spike Milligan

I don't think much of this one!

James Joyce's response when asked what he thought of the next world

Since I got to 80, I've started reading
the Bible a lot more. It's kind of like
cramming for my finals.

Vincent Watson

He's so old that when he orders a
three-minute egg, they ask for the
money up front.

Milton Berle

I used to hate weddings – all those old dears poking me in the stomach and saying 'You're next.' But they stopped all that when I started doing the same to them at funerals.

Gail Flynn

There are worse things in life than death. Have you ever spent an evening with an insurance salesman?

Woody Allen

I want to die young at an
advanced age.

Max Lerner

━━◆━━

I've already lived about 20 years
longer than my life expectancy at the
time I was born. That's a source of
annoyance to a great many people.

Ronald Reagan

In Liverpool, the difference between
a funeral and a wedding is one
less drunk.

Paul O'Grady

If you die in an elevator, be sure to
push the Up button.

Sam Levenson

Errol Flynn died on a 70-foot yacht with a 17-year-old girl. My husband's always wanted to go that way, but he's going to settle for a 17-footer and a 70-year-old.

Mrs Walter Cronkite, wife of retired US journalist

Memorial services are the cocktail parties of the geriatric set.

Harold Macmillan

When I get in a taxi, the first thing
they say is, 'Hello Eric, I thought you
were dead.'

Eric Sykes

My grandmother was a very tough
woman. She buried three husbands
and two of which were just napping.

Rita Rudner

I don't mind dying. Trouble is, you feel so bloody stiff the next day.

George Axelrod

—◆—

I know I can't cheat death, but I can cheat old age.

Darwin Deason

—◆—

An old lady came into the chemist and asked for a bottle of euthanasia. I didn't say anything. I just handed her a bottle of Echinacea.

Lydia Berryman

A stockbroker urged me to buy a stock that would triple its value every year. I told him, 'At my age, I don't even buy green bananas.'

Claude D. Pepper

———◆———

My old mam reads the obituary page everyday but she could never understand how people always die in alphabetical order.

Frank Carson

———◆———

Death is life's way of telling you you're fired.

R. Geis

I don't believe in afterlife, although I am bringing a change of underwear.

Woody Allen

—◆—

They say such nice things about people at their funerals that it makes me sad that I'm going to miss mine by just a few days.

Garrison Kiellor

No one is so old as to think he cannot
live one more year.

Cicero

Life insurance is a weird concept.
You really don't get anything for it. It
works like this: you pay me money and
when you die, I'll pay you money.

Bill Kirchenbauer

I am ready to meet my
Maker. Whether my
Maker is ready for the
ordeal of meeting me is
another matter.

Winston Churchill

We think he's dead, but we're
afraid to ask.

Anonymous Committee Member, of the 79-year-old
Chairman of House Committee, Washington, 1984

All my friends are dead. They're all
in heaven now and they're all up there
mingling with one another. By now,
they are starting to wonder if I might
have gone to the other place.

Teresa Platt

Old age is like waiting in the
departure lounge of life. Fortunately,
we are in England and the train is
bound to be late.

Milton Shulman

———•———

If you think nobody cares whether
you are alive or dead, try missing a
couple of car payments.

Ann Landers

The ageing process is not gradual or gentle. It rushes up, pushes you over and runs off laughing. Dying is a matter of slapstick and prat falls.

John Mortimer

BIRTHDAYS

You're getting old when
the only thing you want
for your birthday is not
to be reminded of it.

Felix Severn

BIRTHDAYS

Age is only a number.

Lexi Starling

———•———

Birthdays are good for you.
Statistics show that the people who
have the most live the longest.

Father Larry Lorenzoni

———•———

When I turned two I was really
anxious, because I'd doubled my age
in a year. I thought, if this keeps up,
by the time I'm six I'll be 90.

Steven Wright

A diplomat is a man who always remembers a woman's birthday but never remembers her age.

Robert Frost

My wife hasn't had a birthday in 4 years. She was born in the year of our Lord-only-knows.

Unknown

A birthday is just the first day of another 365-day journey around the sun. Enjoy the trip.

Unknown

For all the advances in medicine, there is still no cure for the common birthday.

John Glenn

BIRTHDAYS

I'm pleading with my wife to have birthdays again. I don't want to grow old alone.

Rodney Dangerfield

I'm not like Jane Fonda or any of those other women who say how fabulous they think it is to turn 40. I think it's a crock of shit.

Cher

Birthdays are nature's way of telling us to eat more cake.

Jo Brand

The only time a woman wishes she were a year older is when she's having a baby.

Mary Marsh

My wife said to me, 'I don't look 50, do I darling?' I said, 'Not any more.'

Bob Monkhouse

Zsa Zsa Gabor has just celebrated the 41st anniversary of her 39th birthday.

Joan Rivers

BIRTHDAYS

Pushing 40? She's clinging onto it for dear life.

Ivy Compton-Burnett

By the time I lit the last candle on my birthday cake, the first one had gone out.

George Burns at 80

He had too many birthdays.

Andy Marx explaining the cause of his father Groucho's death in 1977

Eighty is the time of your life when even your birthday suit needs pressing

Bob Hope

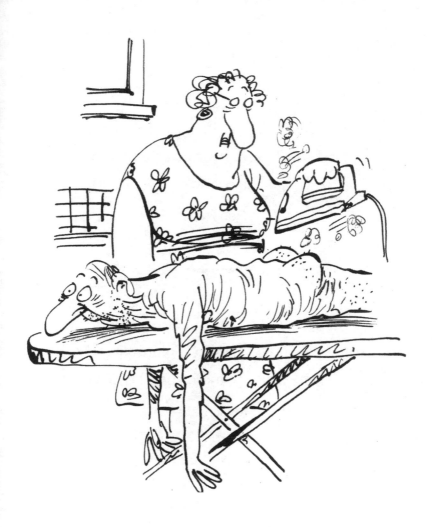

I tried to count the candles on my birthday cake...the heat kept driving me back.

Bob Hope

Birthdays only come once a year unless you're Joan Collins, in which case they only come every four years.

Steven Bauer

One day I said to myself, 'I'm 40.' By the time I recovered from the shock of that discovery I had reached 50.

Simone de Beauvoir

Passing your 80th birthday is a wonderful achievement. You just sit there and it happens.

Angus McBean

FUNFERALLS

Funerals in Ireland are so jolly, they should be called funferalls.

James Joyce

Peter O'Toole looks like he's walking
around just to save funeral expenses.

John Huston

❦

I hate it at weddings when old
relatives tell me, 'You'll be next, love.' I
get my own back at funerals.

Mandy Knight

❦

I refused to attend his funeral, but I
wrote a very nice letter explaining that
I approved of it.

Mark Twain

The reason so many people turned up at Louis B. Mayer's funeral was to make sure that he was dead.

Sam Goldwyn

Movie actors wear dark glasses at funerals to conceal the fact that their eyes aren't red from weeping.

Nunally Jones

Funerals are like bad movies. They last too long, they're overacted, and the end is predictable.

George Burns

I dislike funerals so much I may not even go to my own one.

Brian Behan

Is it worth our while going home?

One old man to another at the funeral of a friend

My father's funeral cost me ten
grand. I buried him in a rented suit.

Red Skelton

I hope you die before me because I
don't want you singing at my funeral.

Spike Milligan to Harry Secombe

No matter how great a man is, the size
of his funeral usually depends on
the weather.

Rosemary Clooney

OH, BITCHERY

In obituaries, 'convivial' means drunk, 'a great raconteur' means crashing bore and 'relishing physical contact' describes a cruel sadist.

Vanora Bennett

I've just learned about his illness.
Let's hope it's nothing trivial.

Irvin S. Cobb

———•———

Age cannot wither him, nor exhaust
his infinite mendacity.

Tom Collins

———•———

Tonight we honour a man old enough
to be his own father.

Red Skelton introducing George Burns

Every morning I read the obituary page over breakfast. If I'm not in it, I get up.

Benjamin Franklin

———◆———

They say you shouldn't say nothing about the dead unless it's good. He's dead. Good.

Jackie Mabley

ELDERLY MUSINGS

There are many mysteries in old age but the greatest, surely, is this: in those adverts for walk-in bathtubs, why doesn't all the water gush out when you get in?

Alan Coren

And in the end, it's not the years in your life that count. It's the life in your years.

Abraham Lincoln

About the only thing that comes to us without effort is old age.

Gloria Pitzer

When you win, you're an old pro. When you lose, you're an old man.

Charley Conerly

Life's tragedy is that we get old too soon and wise too late.

Benjamin Franklin

Nobody loves life like him who is growing old.

Sophocles

One should never make one's debut in a scandal. One should reserve that to give interest to one's old age.

Oscar Wilde

Oft from shrivelled skin comes
useful counsel.

Saemund

Life is a moderately good play with a
badly written third act.

Truman Capote

A lady of a certain age, which means
certainly aged.

Lord Byron

Anyone can get old. All you have to do is live long enough.

Groucho Marx

It's true, some wines improve with age. But only if the grapes were good in the first place.

Abigail Van Buren, (Pauline Phillips) and Jeanne Phillips

Grandchildren don't make a man
feel old; it's the knowledge that he's
married to a grandmother.

G. Norman Collie

Wisdom doesn't necessarily come
with age. Sometimes age just shows
up all by itself.

Tom Wilson

May you live all the days of your life.

Jonathan Swift

By the time I have money to burn, my
fire will have burnt out.

Unknown

Life can only be understood
backwards, but it must be
lived forwards.

Soren Kierkegaard

Resolve to be tender with the young, compassionate with the aged, sympathetic with the striving, and tolerant with the weak and the wrong. Sometime in your life you will have been all of these.

Dr Robert H. Goddard

———•———

Growing old is like being increasingly penalised for a crime you haven't committed.

Anthony Powell

I go slower as time goes faster.

Mason Cooley

———————

Half our life is spent trying to find
something to do with the time we have
rushed through life trying to save.

Will Rogers

———————

Men who are orthodox when they are
young are in danger of being middle-
aged all their lives.

Walter Lippmann

When I was young, I thought that money was the most important thing in life; now that I am old, I know it is.

Oscar Wilde

Well enough for old folks to rise early, because they have done so many mean things all their lives they can't sleep anyhow.

Mark Twain

I don't believe one grows older. I think that what happens early on in life is that at a certain age one stands still and stagnates.

T. S. Eliot

I am long on ideas, but short on time. I
expect to live to be only about
a hundred.

Thomas Alva Edison

Age is something that doesn't matter,
unless you are a cheese.

Billie Burke

Old age is the verdict of life.

Amelia E. Barr

Growing old is something you do if you're lucky.

Groucho Marx

❖

Age wrinkles the body. Quitting wrinkles the soul.

Douglas MacArthur

❖

God gives nuts to those with no teeth.

Unknown

You can't turn back the clock. But you can wind it up again.

Bonnie Prudden

Life is a funny thing that happens to you on the way to the grave.

Quentin Crisp

❦

Very few people do anything creative after the age of 35. The reason is that very few people do anything creative before the age of 35.

Joel Hildebrand

SOBERING THOUGHTS

The three ages of man
are under-age, over-age
and average.

Herbert Prochnow

Science has salvaged scrap metal and even found vitamins and valuable oils in refuse, but old people are extravagantly wasted.

Anzia Yezierska

People ought to be either one of two things: young or dead.

Dorothy Parker

For a while you're a veteran, and then you're just old.

Lance Alworth

I'm very uncomfortable living in a world where the Pope is 25 years younger than I am.

Billy Wilder in 1993

———◆———

The living are the dead on holiday.

Maurice Maeterlinck

———◆———

Old age is life's parody.

Simone De Beauvoir

I know I'm going to die because my birth certificate has an expiry date on it.

Steven Wright

There comes a time in every man's life where he must make way for an older man.

Reginald Maudling

WOMEN AND MEN

Trouble is, by the time
you can read a girl like a
book, your library card
has expired.

Milton Berle

Few women admit their age. Few men act theirs.

Unknown

An archaeologist is the best husband a woman can have. The older she gets the more interested he is in her.

Agatha Christie

When women enter middle age, it gives men a pause.

Unknown

The best years of a woman's life –
the ten years between 39 and 40.

Unknown

Women are not forgiven for ageing.
Robert Redford's lines of distinction
are my old-age wrinkles.

Jane Fonda

The lovely thing about being 40 is
that you can appreciate
25 year-old men.

Colleen McCullough

My husband's idea of a good night
out is a good night in.

Maureen Lipman

A woman's always younger than a
man of equal years.

Elizabeth Barrett Browning

A woman is as old as she looks
before breakfast.

Edgar Watson Howe

———•———

When I passed 40 I dropped
pretense, 'cause men like women who
got some sense.

Maya Angelou

337

Whatever you may look like, marry a
man your own age – as your beauty
fades, so will his eyesight.

Phyllis Diller

The best way to get a husband to do
anything is to suggest that he is too
old to do it.

Felicity Parker

Age to women is like Kryptonite
to Superman.

Kathy Lette

WORDS AND MUSIC

A 'Selected Poems'
anthology is like a clock
awarded by an affable
but faintly impatient
employer.

Sean O'Brien

I dislike modern memoirs. They're generally written by people who have either lost their memories or have never done anything worth remembering.

Oscar Wilde

—◆—

After a certain age, a poet's main rival is the poet he used to be.

William Logan

—◆—

You eventually reach an age where every sentence bumps into one you wrote 30 years ago.

John Updike

I was asked how we should celebrate
Harold Pinter's fiftieth Birthday. I
should have suggested a
minute's silence.

Alan Bennett

I'm old enough to remember Elvis the
first time he was alive.

Noel V. Ginnity

When I was young we didn't have
MTV. We had to take drugs and go
to concerts.

Steven Pearl

341

She was an ageing singer who had to take every note above 'A' with her eyebrows.

Montague Glass

I was a veteran before I was a teenager.

Michael Jackson

The best epitaph for a blues singer
would be, 'Didn't Wake Up
This Morning'.

Burl Ives

People like their blues singers dead.

Janis Joplin

People tell me I'm a legend. In other words, a has-been.

Bob Dylan

EXPERIENCE, MISTAKES AND ADVICE

Experience is a terrible
teacher who sends
horrific bills.

Unknown

For the first half of your life, people tell you what you should do; for the second half, they tell you what you should have done.

Richard Needham

❧—•—❧

I'll never make the mistake of being 70 again.

Casey Stengel

❧—•—❧

If I had my life to live over again, I'd make the same mistakes, only sooner.

Tallulah Bankhead

If I had my life to live over again, I'd be
a plumber.

Albert Einstein

❦

Age is a high price to pay
for maturity.

Tom Stoppard

❦

The man who views the world at 50
the same as he did at 20 has wasted
30 years of his life.

Muhammad Ali

My greatest regret is not knowing at 30 what I knew about women at 60.

Arthur Miller

I get to be a kid now, because I wasn't a kid when I was supposed to be one. But in some ways, I'm like an old woman – lived it, seen it, done it, been there, have the T-shirt.

Drew Barrymore

Autumn is mellower, and what we lose in flowers, we more than gain in fruits.

Samuel Butler

I used to have a sign over my computer that read 'Old dogs can learn new tricks', but lately I sometimes ask myself how many more new tricks I want to learn. Wouldn't it just be easier to be outdated?

Ram Dass

Cherish all your happy moments: they make a fine cushion for old age.

Christopher Morley

—•—

You don't appreciate a lot of stuff in school until you get older. Little things like being spanked every day by a middle-aged woman: stuff you pay good money for in later life.

Emo Philips

—•—

Whenever I get down about life going by too quickly, what helps me is a little mantra that I repeat to myself: at least I'm not a fruit fly.

Ray Romano

We learn from experience that men never learn anything from experience.

George Bernard Shaw

The post office has a great charm at one point of our lives. When you have lived to my age you will begin to think letters are never worth going through the rain for.

Jane Austen

A prune is an experienced plum.

John Trattner

I have lived in the world just long enough to look carefully the second time into those things that I am most certain of the first time.

Josh Billings

I advise you to go on living solely to enrage those who are paying your annuities. It is the only pleasure I have left.

François Voltaire

When I was young, I was told: 'You'll see when you're 50.' I'm 50 and I haven't seen a thing.

Erik Satie

When people tell you how young you look, they are also telling you how old you are.

Cary Grant

Life is too short to learn German.

Richard Porson

As I grow older, I pay less attention to what men say. I just watch what they do.

Andrew Carnegie

Just remember, once
you're over the hill, you
begin to pick up speed.

Charles M. Schulz

Experience is a comb life gives you
after you lose your hair.

Judith Stern

—••—

The time to begin most things is ten
years ago.

Mignon McLaughlin

—••—

If you resolve to give up smoking,
drinking and loving, you don't actually
live longer. It just seems longer.

Clement Freud

Never put off until tomorrow what
you can do the day after.

Louis Safian

———◆———

A woman should never give birth after
35. Thirty-five is enough kids
for anyone.

Gracie Allen

———◆———

I got on well by talking. Death could
not get a word in edgeways, grew
discouraged, and travelled on.

Louise Erdrich

I asked my doctor what I should do after having a pacemaker put in. He said, 'Keep paying your electricity bill.'

Roger Moore

Don't complain about growing old.
Many are denied the privilege.

Somerset Maugham

—◆—

Avoid school reunions. The last man
I met who was at school with me had a
long white beard and no teeth.

P.G. Wodehouse

—◆—

It's not how old you are, it's how
you're old.

Brian Blessed

The only thing for old age is a brave face, a good tailor and comfortable shoes.

Alan Ayckbourn

Most people like the old days best – they were younger then.

Unknown

Nothing is more responsible for the good old days than a bad memory.

Franklin Pierce Adams

It becomes increasingly easy, as you get older, to drown in nostalgia.

Ted Koppel

———⋅———

Sometimes when a man recalls the good old days, he's really thinking of his bad young days.

Unknown

EXIT LINES: FAMOUS LAST WORDS

Dear World, I am leaving because I am bored... Good luck.

Suicide note of George Sanders

Either that wallpaper goes or I do.

Oscar Wilde

No flowers please, just caviar.

Jennifer Paterson

Don't let it end like this. Tell them I said something.

Pancho Villa

Doctor, do you think it could've been the sausage?

Paul Claudel

Keep Paddy behind the mixer.

Building tycoon Sir Alfred McAlpine

I told you I was ill.

Spike Milligan

Last Will and Testament: I, being of
sound mind, have spent every penny.

Ray Ellington

❧

Quick – save the dessert.

Paulette Brillat-Savarin

They couldn't hit an elephant at
this dist-

General John Sedgwick

This is no time for making
new enemies.

Voltaire after a priest had asked him to renounce the
devil on his deathbed

Dear Elise, seek younger friends. I am extinct.

George Bernard Shaw

I've just had 18 whiskies. I think that's a record.

Dylan Thomas

Is there one who understands me?

James Joyce

All in all I'd prefer to be in
Philadelphia.

W. C. Fields

If this is dying, I don't think much of it.

Lytton Strachey

I should never have switched from
scotch to martinis.

Humphrey Bogart

THE BRIGHT SIDE

Every day I beat my
own previous record
for the number of
consecutive days I've
stayed alive.

George Carlin

I woke up this morning and I was still alive so I'm pretty cheerful.

Spike Milligan at 79

❧

We are always the same age inside.

Gertrude Stein

❧

Even if there's snow on the roof, it doesn't mean the fire has gone out in the furnace.

John Diefenbaker

I do not call myself old yet. Not till a young woman offers me her seat will that tragedy really be mine.

E. V. Lucas

To be 70 years young is sometimes far more cheerful and hopeful than to be 40 years old.

Oliver Wendell Holmes

Since I got to be 65, I look better, feel better, make love better and I never lied better.

George Burns

W. C. Fields has a profound respect
for old age. Especially when
it's bottled.

Gene Fowler

My grandmother is over 80 and still
doesn't need glasses. Drinks right
out of the bottle.

Henry Youngman

You know you're getting old when
a four-letter word for something
pleasurable two people can do in bed
is R-E-A-D.

Denis Norden

One of the many pleasures of old age is giving things up.

Malcolm Muggeridge

I smoke 10 to 15 cigars a day, at my age I have to hold on to something.

George Burns

Jameson's Irish Whiskey really does improve with age: the older I get the more I like it.

Bob Monkhouse

When you get to 52 food becomes more important than sex.

Prue Leith

I'm at the age where food has taken the place of sex in my life. In fact, I've just had a mirror put over my kitchen table.

Rodney Dangerfield

I always make a point of starting the day at 6 a.m. with champagne. It goes straight to the heart and cheers one up. White wine won't do. You need the bubbles.

John Mortimer

EPITAPHS

You can count for as
long as you like, but I'm
not getting up this time.

Former world boxing champion Jim Watt's
suggestion

The defence rests.

Suggested epitaph for a lawyer

❧

Here lies Harry Secombe until further notice.

Harry Secombe's suggestion

❧

Jesus Christ – is that the time already?

Billy Connolly's suggestion

Excuse my dust.

Dorothy Parker

On my gravestone I'd like them to put, 'He didn't know what he was doing'.

Terry Wogan

I want my epitaph to be what I once read on my dry cleaning receipt: 'It distresses us to return work that is not perfect'.

Peter O'Toole

Here lies my husband – stiff at last.

Ernest Forbes' suggestion for a bitter wife

382

YOUTH V. OLD AGE

The old begin to complain of the conduct of the young when they themselves are no longer able to set a bad example.

François de la Rochefoucauld

An old timer is one who remembers when we counted our blessings instead of our calories.

Unknown

❧

I am not young enough to know everything.

Oscar Wilde

❧

Youth is a wonderful thing. What a crime to waste it on children.

George Bernard Shaw

A man has reached middle age when he is warned to slow down by his doctor instead of the police.

Unknown

Old age realises the dreams of youth: look at Dean Swift; in his youth he built an asylum for the insane, in his old age he was himself an inmate.

Soren Kierkegaard

Young men want to be faithful, and are not; old men want to be faithless, and cannot.

Oscar Wilde

Twenty-four years ago, Madam, I was incredibly handsome. The remains of it are still visible through the rift of time. I was so handsome that women became spellbound when I came into view. In San Francisco, in rainy seasons, I was frequently mistaken for a cloudless day.

Mark Twain

I never dared to be radical when young for fear it would make me conservative when old.

Robert Frost

The elderly don't drive that badly; they're just the only ones with time to do the speed limit.

Jason Love

I have now gotten to the age when I
must prove that I'm just as good as
I never was.

Rex Harrison

Young people don't know what age
is, and old people forget what
youth was.

Irish proverb

The young man knows the rules but the old man knows the exceptions.

Oliver Wendell Holmes

In youth, we ran into difficulties, in old age difficulties run into us.

Josh Billings, pen name of US humorist Henry Wheeler Shaw

I have everything I had 20 years ago, only it's all a little bit lower.

Gypsy Rose Lee

In youth the days are short and the years are long; in old age the years are short and the days are long.

Nikita Ivanovich Panin

In some ways, I never outgrew my adolescence. I wake up in the morning and think, 'Oh my God, I'm late for a math test!' But then I say, 'Wait a minute. I'm 40.'

Daniel Clowes

One of the many things nobody ever tells you about middle age is that it's a nice change from being young.

William Feather

The old age of an eagle
is better than the youth
of a sparrow.

Proverb

From the earliest times the old have rubbed it into the young that they are wiser than they, and before the young had discovered what nonsense this was they were old too, and it profited them to carry on the imposture.

Somerset Maugham

Youth would be an ideal state if it came a little later in life.

Herbert Asquith, Earl of Oxford

Age is not different from earlier life as long as you're sitting down.

Malcolm Cowley

The old believe everything; the middle-aged suspect everything; the young know everything.

Oscar Wilde

People want you to be like you were in 1969. They want you to be, because otherwise their youth goes with you.

Mick Jagger

Boys will be boys and so will a lot of middle-aged men.

Kin Hubbard

Youth is when you're allowed to stay up late on New Year's Eve. Middle age is when you're forced to.

Bill Vaughn

———•———

I am getting older in a country where a major religion is the Church of Acne.

Bill Cosby

———•———

I used to dread getting older because I thought I would not be able to do all the things I wanted to do, but now that I am older I find that I don't want to do them.

Nancy Astor on her 80th birthday

One day a bachelor, the next a grampa. What is the secret of the trick? How did I get so old so quick?

Ogden Nash

When you are dissatisfied and would like to go back to your youth... Think of algebra.

Will Rogers

The denunciation of the young greatly assists the circulation of the blood.

Logan Pearsall Smith

Never raise your hand
to your children. It
leaves your midsection
unprotected.

Robert Orben

The old-fashioned respect for the young is fast dying out.

Oscar Wilde

What is more enchanting than the voices of young people when you can't hear what they're saying?

Logan Pearsall Smith

Always pat children on the head
whenever you meet them, just in case
they happen to be yours.

Augustus John

Women who remember their first
kiss now have daughters who can't
remember their first husbands.

Henny Youngman

There are only two things a child will share willingly: communicable diseases and his mother's age.

Benjamin Spock

The trouble with the music teenagers listen to these days is that you can't tell when the record is worn out.

Stanley Davis

The dead might as well try to speak to the living as the old to the young.

Willa Cather

Youth is a disease from which we all recover.

Dorothy Fuldheim

The young always have the same problem – how to rebel and conform at the same time. They have now solved this by defying their parents and copying one another.

Quentin Crisp

There's nothing wrong with teenagers that reasoning with them won't aggravate.

Jean Kerr

CHECKING OUT TIME

Dying is the most
embarrassing thing that
can happen to you,
because someone else
has to take care of all
your details.

Andy Warhol

Only the young die good.

Oliver Herford

Save energy. Get cremated
with a friend.

Spike Milligan

I could never bear to be buried with
people to whom I had never
been introduced.

Norman Parkinson

Dying can damage your health.
Every coffin should contain a
Government Health Warning.

Spike Milligan

The good die young because they
see no sense in living if you have
to be good.

John Barrymore

Old florists don't die, they just make
other arrangements.

Nigel Rees

Reports of my death are greatly
exaggerated.

Mark Twain

He says it's a marvellous business... In 30 years he's never had a customer ask for a refund.

Hal Roach on an uncle's business as an undertaker

Committing suicide is the last thing I'd ever do.

Kenny Everett

If Shaw and Einstein couldn't beat death, what chance have I got?

Mel Brooks

Last month my aunt passed away. She was cremated. We think that's what did it.

Jonathan Katz

You live and learn, then you die and forget it all.

Nöel Coward

An undertaker is the last man to let you down.

Danny Cummings

Immortality is a long shot, I admit. But somebody has to be first.

Bill Cosby

OLD REMNANTS

As long as a woman can look ten years younger than her daughter, she is perfectly satisfied.

Oscar Wilde

A geriatric is a German cricketer who captures three successive wickets.

George Coote

I attribute my great age to the simple fact that I was born a very long time ago.

John Gielgud

There is something worse than growing old – remaining a child.

Cesare Pavese

There are no old people nowadays. They're either 'wonderful for their age' or dead.

Mary Pettibone Poole

The older I get, the more passionate I
become about fewer things.

Brendan Kennelly

Every morning when you're 93, you
wake up and say to yourself,
'What – again?'

Ben Travers

Have you enjoyed this book? If so, why not write a review on your favourite website?

Thanks very much for buying this Summersdale book.

www.summersdale.com